I0453734

Sweet Ninety

A Discovery of Belonging

Sweet Ninety

A Discovery of Belonging

Meredith Woods Potter

Long River Books
Masterful Person Company Publishing
mpcpublishing.com

© 2024 Meredith Woods Potter

All rights reserved. No part of this publication may be reproduced, distributed, or transmitted in any form or by any means, including photocopying, recording, or other electronic or mechanical methods, without the prior written permission of the publisher, except in the case of brief quotations embodied in critical reviews and certain other noncommercial uses permitted by copyright law. For permission requests, write to the publisher, addressed "Attention: Permissions Coordinator," at the address above.

ISBN: 978-1-962771-21-4

Library of Congress Control Number: 2024923192

This is a memoir. The events and people herein are portrayed to the best of the author's memory. It reflects the author's present recollections of experiences over time.

Typeface: Garamond 14p.

Cover design and illustration by Roane Furlong.

Table of Contents

The First Words

The First Words

My family requested, encouraged, and then implored me to write the stories of my life. As the matriarch of the family, I now held our life and history. My first attempts at recording my life resulted in a Shutterfly "picture book" titled "The Book of Meredith." Additional books followed: "Remembering Tak" (The life of the young Japanese boy, who became our "godbrother" when he came into our household as a teenager), "Our Tokyo Years," and the special record of my sister Sarah's and my cruise up the Danube titled "The Sail of Two Sisters." My oldest son, Willis, the genealogist in the family, collaborated with me to produce The

Woods Family and Our Quaker Roots. It recorded the history and biographies of our Woods forebears and cleared up some mis-remembered family stories. But much was left to record for grandchildren and great-grandchildren.

Soon after moving to Jubilation, a retirement community in Fredericksburg, Virginia, I began to attend a weekly writing class given by Jen Furlong, published author, actor, and founder of Masterful Person Company Publishing. She encouraged me to write short story accounts of incidents in my life and taught me how to do it. This book is really a collection of those short stories. I am grateful to the participants in that class who listened to and critiqued many of the early drafts. I am particularly indebted to fellow writer, Bob McMains, who has read and offered incredibly helpful insights and suggestions for each of the stories included in this volume. His friendship, encouragement, and non-judgmental feedback kept me writing. I am also indebted to Tabitha Pollardson, who has been such a helpful editor, correcting grammar, offering suggestions, and helping me hone my writing skills.

These stories are my recollections, and I take full responsibility for the accuracy and truthfulness as I remember the events. As for the inevitable corrections and criticisms of my siblings, who experienced some of these accounts, I can only shrug my shoulders, and say, "I'm sorry," reminding them at age 90, they're lucky I can still remember their names and birthdays, much less the events herein recorded.

Part 1

Young and Just Begun
1934-1946

My Thumb

I'm not sure why sucking my thumb became such a big deal. I loved the taste of my thumb; I loved the comfort it gave me when I was tired, or hungry, or angry at my sister, or sad, or happy, or whenever. Mother tried everything. Bribery came first--but the quarter didn't convince me. Next, she tried having me wear a glove. I didn't care. I responded by sucking the other thumb – it tasted about the same. So Mother put both hands in gloves; I sucked a hole in one of the gloves. In desperation, Mother painted my thumbs with iodine. I sucked off the iodine. My mother, convinced she had poisoned me, called the doctor. Then she tried shame. "Girls who are big sisters don't suck their thumbs."

"Why not?"

"Girls big enough for school don't suck their thumbs."

"Yes, they do."

Then, "Girls big enough to read don't suck their thumbs." But that argument didn't make any sense to me at all. Learning to read provided me with some additional entertainment to my thumb sucking.

Mother became more and more frustrated with my thumb sucking, especially after the birth of my sister Barbie. Barbie didn't help matters, showing no signs of recognizing her thumb or the joy it might give her. I didn't understand how my thumb had anything to do with having a baby sister. I had no idea why Mother obsessed so over my thumb. After all, it was my thumb, not hers.

In desperation, when I turned nine, she took me to see a special "doctor." Each week, we took the streetcar to the clinic for our weekly chat. I couldn't understand why mother kept crying, telling the doctor how she had failed as a parent. She had stopped nursing me too soon. She had not paid enough attention to me after Barbie's arrival. She didn't understand the needs of her oldest child.

After every session, Mother cried most of the streetcar ride home. I held the book, reading in both hands, fearing that if I put my thumb in my mouth, Mother would cry even harder.

Then one day, Mother told me we were going to see a new doctor. I hid in my room and sucked my thumb in dreaded anticipation. Mother told me about the new doctor, Dr. Von Something-or-other. I prepared for another tall, stern white-haired man. But Dr. Von Something-or-other turned out to be a woman, about the size and age of my mother. She wore her hair in a funny knot at the back of her head – kind of like the way my grandmother wore her hair. She wore a white coat, like the other doctor, but she also wore funny, tall black shoes that seemed to lace forever.

I stared at her; she stared back. I put my thumb in my mouth– more to see how this new doctor might respond than for comfort. She continued to look at me. I kept sucking my thumb. Then suddenly I became frightened as I looked at Mother and pleaded, "I want to go home." Dr. Von Something-or-other cleared her throat. "Vell, my *kleinkind*," she said. "You and I have things to talk about." I looked up at her, took my thumb out of my mouth, and began to cry. I had sucked my thumb for the last time.

The Truth, the Real Truth

As soon as my younger sister Barbie learned to talk, she became the family's self-designated foremost authority. She not only held an opinion about everything imaginable, she stomped her right foot, clutched her waist with both hands, and declared her point of view with total conviction. She was adorable: curly chestnut braids tied with ribbons to match her dress, bangs that bounced as she declared her latest "fact," and the biggest, brownest eyes of any family member.

By the time she turned three, she began to spin more and more tales, which I couldn't believe our mother actually accepted as fact – particularly when Barbie's account of our latest altercation often got me in trouble. "After all," Mother always responded, "you are the big sister, Meredith. I expect better behavior from you."

One day Barbie came home from Sunday school and proudly announced at the Sunday dinner table, "We learned to sing 'Jesus Loves Me' in Chinese today in Sunday school."

I responded immediately. "Liar, liar, pants on fire."

Mother said, "Shush," and then asked Barbie to explain. With studied solemnity Barbie replied, "A missionary came to our classroom this morning and taught us the song."

"Liar!" I shouted again. As Dad expressed interest, I began to fear that maybe our parents actually believed her. I tried to say that if there really had been a missionary in Sunday school, I'd have known about it. Again, Mother shushed me. So, I decided to call my sister's bluff: "Well, then sing it for us," I demanded. With a twinkle in her eyes, she began to sing, "Hang-lock-a-to-ee."

I protested, "That's not Chinese!" My protests went unheard as Dad's laughter drowned out Mother's clapping.

The years went by, and I became less and less able to tolerate my cute but conniving little sister. She never did anything wrong; she never got punished; her explanations of her behavior were always so carefully crafted, they came across as almost believable. I was always the guilty one, the one held responsible for our fights and our misbehaviors.

One day I had absolutely had it. Mother had asked: "Who started the fight?" Barbie of course had pointed to me, saying, "She started it when she hit me back." About to be punished for the umpteenth time, I grabbed her by the pigtails, whispering threats of wringing her neck. Before she could scream for Mother, I threatened her, "If you don't tell Mother the truth, I'm going to wring your neck." She looked up at me adoringly with those big brown eyes and asked, "You want me to tell you the truth?" Still grabbing hold of her, I nodded sternly. "The **real** truth?" she asked.

Barbie and Meredith - when not fighting

The Repair

"Apologize to your mother, young lady!" Dad's voice, calm but stern.

"No." My response, both loud and defiant.

"You heard me. You don't talk to your mother like that."

"But it wasn't my fault," I replied, defensively.

"I'm not talking about you and your sister. You don't talk to your mother like that. Apologize. Now."

"No," I repeated, as I ran to my room, shut and locked the door.

"Meredith. Come back here. You don't run off when I'm talking to you." Dad's voice grew louder.

"No," I shouted from behind my bedroom door.

I heard the knob rattle. "I'm not coming out."

And then I saw my father's shoulder as the door broke loose from its hinges, pieces of the shattered door frame falling to the floor. I stared at my father in astonishment, not knowing what to expect. He stared at me and then he stared at the door. Silence.

He cleared his throat, and in a controlled tone of voice, said, "Go to the garage and bring me the toolbox. I'll also need the tape measure from the kitchen drawer." I quickly did as I had been told, running to the garage and returning with the toolbox in hand. I handed him a screwdriver, still not sure what was going to happen. He unscrewed the broken wood from each hinge and pried the broken door frame away from the threshold.

"I'll need to write down some measurements. Go get paper and a pencil," he said. Handing him the tape measure, I got paper and pencil from my desk as he dictated the size of molding needed to replace the broken door frame. He left the room and returned with his coat and hat. "Get your coat. We need to go to the hardware store." I followed him to the car.

I walked behind him into the hardware store and to the building materials section. He asked, "What were those measurements?" I took the sheet of paper out of my pocket and repeated the size needed and he measured a pre-painted piece of wood. "Does this look about right?" I nodded. He paid for the board and a box of small nails. We got back into the car and rode home in silence.

Slowly we worked together, handing each other parts and tools – in much the same way as we had built radios together - until the frame had been replaced, and the door rehung. Only on this day we worked in silence, and every time he turned toward me, I flinched, not knowing what to expect, since Dad had never even raised his voice at me in the past. I got the broom and dustpan, without being asked, and swept up the last evidence of the broken door and what had happened.

After I had finished cleaning up and taken the broken pieces of wood to the garbage, Dad looked me straight in the eye and said, "I promise that's the last time I'll lose my temper with you."

As my eyes met those of my father, I replied, "Me, too."

Dad and Meredith in the 90s – still best buddies

Pearl Harbor

It was Sunday morning, December 7, 1941. As a dispatcher for Santa Fe Trailways, Dad's job entailed assigning the buses going to and from Camp Callan Army Training Center near La Jolla, California. Dad seldom worked on Sunday mornings. But today, the beginning of the Christmas holiday, Dad needed to load the young recruits on buses as they headed home for leave. Dad didn't think loading soldiers on the buses would take more than an hour or two, so he asked me if I wanted to go with him. Of course! I adored my father and loved every minute I spent with him. I jumped up and down, grabbed my coat from Mother, and pulled open the door of the company Ford, whose red and yellow paint job advertised "Santa Fe Trailways."

Our trip to the army base took only thirty minutes. Dad drove into the base, showing his pass, and parked the car in front of the bus depot. The red and yellow Santa Fe buses, marked San Diego, Los Angeles, San Francisco, San Antonio, and Denver, were lined up in rows in preparation for the soldiers' boarding. The uniformed soldiers gathered nervously, luggage bags on their shoulders, waiting for their bus number to be called. Dad took me inside and we sat at the lunch counter in the main waiting room. He ordered me a tuna fish sandwich and root beer. Quite a treat. He told me, "It won't take me long to board the soldiers on their buses. Eat your sandwich and wait for me here." I gazed out a window, watching him speak to the bus drivers and point soldiers into different lines, then turned to my sandwich.

I was still eating when Dad returned. As he looked at the menu, a crackling sound filled the room as loudspeakers blared a message, snapping all heads to attention: "Attention, all military personnel. The Japanese have attacked Pearl Harbor. All personnel are to report to their duty stations. This is not a drill. I repeat. All personnel are to report to their duty stations. This is not a drill."

Dad picked up my jacket from the back of the stool. "Get into the car. We have to catch the buses." I grabbed my uneaten half sandwich and ran after him to the car. Our car roared out of the parking lot and through the gate onto the highway. Confused, scared but a bit excited by going so fast, I asked: "Why do we have to catch the buses?"

"Because the soldiers have to return to the base."

"Why?"

"Because they may have to go to war."

"Why?" Dad didn't try to answer this last question. We passed one bus. Dad honked the car horn and motioned the driver to the side of the road. I laughed at the car's bus horn! My mood grew immediately somber as Dad hollered, "Return to base NOW." We pulled back onto the highway until we spotted another bus. This time Dad only honked and flew past the bus. I had never ridden in a car going so fast. We passed two or three more buses, honking as Dad tried to get each driver's attention. When we had gotten way ahead of the buses, Dad pulled to the side of the road and shouted at me, "Stay in the car." He grabbed his jacket from the back seat and ran into the middle of the highway. He began to wave his jacket as if it were a semaphore. Back and forth.

The first bus approached. I was terrified the bus was going to run over my father. But Dad waved it to the side of the road and spoke quickly to the bus driver. The bus crossed the highway and headed back in the other direction. Dad kept waving as each bus approached. Each bus crossed the highway and headed back to the base.

Finally, Dad came back to our car. He didn't say anything. I looked at him. Tears were pouring from his eyes and onto his cheeks. "Those poor men," he mumbled. That was the first time I ever saw my father cry.

Barbie couldn't pronounce the letter "l" so we taught her to look at this picture taken of Dad serving his country during World War II and recite: "I love a long lanky lad living in London in the lap of luxury."

Torch Lake

My mother's two sisters and their husbands owned a cottage together on beautiful Torch Lake in Michigan. Every summer, our family looked forward to visiting Aunt Edith and Uncle Nelson and Aunt Emily and Uncle Art at the lake. The trip to Torch Lake seemed to take forever, but Uncle Nelson made the trip fun by entertaining us with his antics. As we got into the car, Uncle Nelson always donned a French beret and instantly become "Pierre le Pete." He told one joke after another as we wended our way north. When we made the traditional "pea soup" stop at Bill Knapp's restaurant in New Buffalo, he ordered his lunch with a funny accent, blowing the words out through his nose. We giggled until we got older; then we feigned embarrassment.

After hours – that seemed forever –our bodies sensed the lake even before we could see it. We sucked the lake breeze into our nostrils as the car bumped over the railroad tracks, and down the lane. "Oh, look, the Smiths painted their cottage again," observed Aunt Emily. "You don't suppose they sold it," replied Uncle Art. Then into the driveway. We arrived at the cottage.

We opened the back door that led into the kitchen. The smell of mildew almost knocked us over. We ran to open windows, as Dad proclaimed once again: "This year we've got to replace that damn smelly couch." Mother shushed him for swearing in front of us children.

We carried our clothes to the screened-in porch where the children slept as Uncle Nelson lit the fire from the dry logs left on the hearth last summer. As the smell of burning logs and pinecones filled the air, we breathed deeply. With that first deep breath, I always felt a deep refreshment – something I felt as a child, but only identified later in life as "spiritual renewal."

Chores done. I escaped at last, through the porch, onto the deck, and down the path to the boat dock. Tomorrow I'd get out the canoe, but right now I was content to sit at the water's edge, shoes and socks on the deck, dangling my feet in the frigid water of Torch Lake. I struggled, wanting to keep my feet in the cold, cold water as the pain crept up my feet, past my ankles until the icy water caused my whole body to shiver. Pulling my feet out of the water, I concentrated on renewing my acquaintance with our family's beloved lake. Eight miles long and two miles wide, the lake changed colors before my eyes whenever I looked at it.

Each year I looked at the lake as if for the first time. I saw the smoke from a fireplace across the lake, the dust from a car driving along the lake's foot. I couldn't hear the family's voices; I couldn't hear any cars. Only Torch Lake produced such a special silence. A silence that soaked into my soul.

Wonderful flowers grew in the garden that once housed the *casita* (Uncle Art's attempt to describe the outhouse in Esperanto), later replaced in by indoor plumbing. I can still remember my grandmother drawing water from the lake as she cooked dinner on a wood stove. In later years, my younger siblings benefited from running water, a real kitchen and bathroom.

Years later when I traveled to Torch Lake with my own children, Aunt Emily and Uncle Art dressed up in the same Indian outfits that I remembered from my childhood. My boys heard the same stories, received the same quarter pulled out of their ears by their great-uncle, the Indian chief. What they missed in their days at Torch Lake was Pierre le Pete, only a legend by the time they were born.

When only Aunt Edith remained of the aunts and uncles, my parents sold the Torch Lake property. My siblings and I have always wondered why we weren't offered the chance to acquire it – to become beloved aunts and uncles, perhaps even bringing a new Pierre le Pete to the next generation of Woods children. Woods children to complain about, but not replace, the moldy couch. Woods children who might have had their souls refreshed by the gentle breezes, and so many family traditions.

Aunt Edith at the Torch Lake cottage

No Time to Say Goodbye

In my young years, we moved often, but no matter where we lived, we took the train every summer to Chicago to visit our grandparents. Grandmother and Grandfather Woods lived only a block from the Museum of Science and Industry, and almost every day Pop (as we called our grandfather) took us to the museum. I particularly loved the submarine and the coal mine. Those summers in Chicago provided stability and predictability through our many moves, and sometimes, the bridge from one home location to the next.

When we made the trip to Chicago the summer of 1946, Dad had returned home from overseas Army duty, and our reunited family enjoyed our newest home and friends in Albuquerque. Carl lived next door. We walked to school together each day, and he soon became my new best friend. As our Chicago visit ended and we boarded the train toward home, I could hardly wait to share my summer experiences and trips to the museum with Carl.

The train whistle blew as the Albuquerque station platform came into view. I stood up excitedly. Mother's arm reached out in front me. "We're not getting off here. Your Dad has been transferred to San Francisco, so we'll stay on the train which will take us to our new home."

How could that be? Why were we moving again so soon? I had to say goodbye to Carl. As the train stopped, I begged Mother to let me call Carl from the pay phone on the station platform. Wiping back tears, I put a quarter in the phone slot and dialed my best friend. The line was busy. I dialed Carl's number again, and again, and again. Mother opened the phone booth door and took me by the hand. "We have to get back on the train. It's about to leave. Aren't you excited to hear about our new home?"

I sat on the seat in our train compartment and cried. Mother's words failed to console me: "You know, dear, God never closes a door without opening a new door. Let's talk about the new door He's opening for us in San Francisco." I didn't want another of God's "new doors." I didn't want to move again. I didn't want to make new friends. I wanted to see Carl.

What I didn't realize that day on the train as we left Albuquerque were the many of God's new doors yet to unfold in my future. That day on the train platform in Albuquerque became one of many times to come when I didn't get to say goodbye.

Part 2

The Tokyo Years & Coming "Home"

1947-1954

What's in a Name

"You have a baby brother!" Dad grabbed the large carp-shaped windsock, which the servants had gotten "just in case," and hoisted it up the flagpole, following the Japanese custom of announcing the arrival of a boy child. My sisters and I jumped up and down at the news. Charles Palmer Woods – carrying on the Woods legacy of naming the firstborn Charles and attaching the mother's maiden name as his middle name. My father's older sister had been named Caroline, and I never could figure out my grandparents' lack of imagination, naming both their children essentially the same name, until it occurred to me that Caroline, as the first born, was given the feminine form of

Charles. But I still wondered why they repeated essentially the same name when my father arrived three years later.

Our new baby brother became the "Bonnie Prince Charlie" in our family until Great Britain usurped our brother's nickname for their own Charles, heir to the throne, born several months after our own Bonnie Prince. The servants created our brother's lifelong name. They began calling our new-born brother "Boku-chan," which translates to "little user of masculine pronouns," the traditional Japanese nickname for the firstborn son. Our family ultimately Anglicized that nickname to "Bokie," which we still call him today.

When Bokie turned two, Mother and Dad announced that he needed a brother, since he was surrounded by older sisters—"And your baby brother is already on the way!" I couldn't understand why Bokie or any of us needed another brother. And as a junior in high school, it embarrassed me to tell my friends, "My mother is pregnant — again!"

The day came, and my sisters and I waited expectantly for Dad to return from the hospital with news of our new brother's arrival. Bokie, not realizing he would no longer be the baby boy, couldn't have cared less. We heard the car in the driveway. Dad opened the front door and handed his hat to Sachi-san as he removed his shoes. "Well?" we asked.

"You have a new baby sister."

How could that have happened? Mom and Dad planned a brother for Bokie. Surely they knew he didn't need another sister. I certainly didn't need another younger sister!!

My sisters and I sat at the dining room table as Dad asked us to help him pick out a name for the new baby. Obviously, Jonathon—which my parents had chosen—wouldn't work for a girl. We asked Dad how they'd decided all of our names.

"Meredith," Dad began. "You were named after your mother Mary, and my mother Edith."

"How come you didn't name me Mary Edith?"

"We thought Meredith sounded more sophisticated than Mary Edith. But when you were born, we had every intention of calling you Mary."

It took me a while to absorb the thought I might have been Mary.

Barbie piped up. "Where did Barbara come from?"

"Your mother and I picked out Deborah for you, but our close friends named their baby Deborah, so we had to think up a new name for you. Barbara went well with Scott, which we had chosen for your middle name."

Barbie nodded. At least she bore her grandmother's maiden name for a middle name.

Jan and Barb both asked at the same time: "Where did Meredith's middle name come from?"

I spoke up. "I didn't have a middle name until my confirmation. I chose the name Prescott for our great-great-grandfather, Colonel William Prescott, who proclaimed at the Battle of Bunker Hill, 'Don't shoot till you see the whites of their eyes.'"

"Why did you do that?" my sisters asked.

"I thought it was cool — to be named after a revolutionary war ancestor."

Now Jan spoke up. "I know Carolyn, my middle name, is your sister's name, Dad. But where in the world did you get Janess? And why did you saddle me with that weird spelling?"

"Your mother and I both liked Janice, and I chose the Welsh spelling."

"Yeah, right." My sisters and I laughed.

But now we had to choose a name for our newest sister. I liked Margaret — the name I wished I'd been given. We loved Mother's cousin Julie, who lived with us during the war, so we proposed the name Juliana. Back and forth we went. Margaret. Juliana. How to decide? Finally, Dad suggested, "Both those names are great. Why don't I go back to the hospital and let your mother choose between the two?"

We tried to play games while we waited, but one of us kept getting up and running to the window, hoping for Dad to return with the name chosen. Finally, after what seemed like hours, we heard the car in the driveway. Dad, home at last. Margaret or Juliana? We bolted to the front door. "What did Mother decide?" we asked as we hugged Dad, jumping up and down. Dad slowly handed his hat to Sachi-san, took off his shoes, and entered the living room. He sat down in the overstuffed chair. Smiling, he said, "Sarah Elizabeth."

On a Hokkaido Hillside

Gales of laughter and squeals of joy from excited children. Servants trying to gather clothes and respond to orders being shouted in both English and Japanese. Our entire family, including my grandparents visiting from Tucson, prepared to escape the heat of Tokyo with a train trip to the northern Japanese island of Hokkaido.

After four long years serving in the US Army's transportation corps in England during World War II, Dad had barely resumed working for Santa Fe when the US government recruited him to help the Japanese people rebuild their transportation systems that had been decimated by bombs or confiscated for the war effort. Our family joined Dad in Tokyo as soon as "occupation" families were permitted to enter the country, and one hot day during our third summer in our new home, we embarked upon one of many travel adventures to explore the new country we now called "home."

Mother somehow managed to get all of us – servants, grandparents, and kids – and our food and belongings into the two family cars. Did she consciously assign me to the station wagon to care for younger siblings and practice my developing Japanese language skills on the servants, while Mother and Dad and the grandparents rode in comfort, laughing and telling stories in English? How could one family going to one destination manage two distinct cultural journeys – leaving me torn to juggle back and forth between the two?

We boarded the private railcar -- already attached to the train bound for Sendai -- a benefit of Dad's job and position. Possessions stowed in our own little cabins. Schizophrenic chattering of old and young, servants and family, Japanese and English. At fifteen my life seemed a cacophony of sound and sight, being and doing. Only years later did I understand the implications of being an introvert among a raucous family of extroverts. But even as a teenager, I knew my family exhausted me.

Noon. The second day of our trip. Our railcar disengaged from the northbound train, and we rested on a siding on the outskirts of Sendai. I pleaded with Mother: "Please take Grandma and Grandpa and my sisters to the museum in town without me. Sachi-san can handle my baby brother Boku-chan. Let me stay here. I won't go far. I promise." Dad, sensing my need for "alone time," interceded on my behalf. I took off across the meadow. Sitting on the hillside, I gazed at the small village below. School children were playing games on the playing field. I could tell they were singing or shouting, but the gentle breeze carried their voices away into the valley below. I watched them clap their hands as they began to dance together. What summer festival could it be? Too early for the children's Bunkasi cultural festival, or the festival of local deities – neither celebrated in a school yard. What was the holiday today? My joy quickened as my heart began to beat faster. How much I wanted to be part of their field day.

All these thoughts about the children in the valley below intruded into my consciousness, Japanese and English both competing for my attention until at last my thoughts fell silent – a languageless silence. I sat in utter silence watching a silent village; children's silent voices, playing children's silent games. This silent world. So different from my noisy thoughts, my noisy family, my noisy world. True silence at last. Then God's voiceless command came into my consciousness, piercing the worldly silence. The first time I heard God calling me to become a priest.

The Day my Hero was Fired

I picked up my golf ball after three-putting the eighteenth hole and voiced the question that had been troubling my classmates and me for days. "Dad, do you think the conflict in Korea is going to become World War III?"

My father looked at me, somewhat astonished. We usually played golf together on Sunday morning before church. But this particular Wednesday, Dad had a rare midweek day off, so I skipped school so we could enjoy a bonus golf date together. Dad clearly hadn't expected to address the unrest and uncertainty surrounding our lives in Tokyo, but he also didn't dismiss me.

Instead, he asked, "What in the world makes you think that might happen?"

"Our school is so different since all those new students arrived from South Korea last week when their families were evacuated."

I tried to explain what they had been sharing with us. "All the new kids can talk about is what's happening in South Korea; they're all afraid General MacArthur is going to invade North Korea or even China."

Dad nodded. I continued: "They think that General MacArthur and President Truman don't agree about how to end the war. And it sounds to me that they're on President Truman's side." General MacArthur was our school's hero. "I really don't get why the president argued with his general. Why can't they work together to end the war!"

Dad took a deep breath and tried to explain: "President Truman sees the war as a chance to stop communism from spreading into South Korea. But General MacArthur has set his sights on liberating North Korea from communist control."

"I'm confused. It seems to me the war ought to do both. How can you keep communism from coming into South Korea without getting rid of it in North Korea? Isn't that the only way to reunite the north and south?"

"Apparently, President Truman and General MacArthur have quite different strategies for ending the conflict. The president's main concern seems to be to save as many lives as possible, even if that means a ceasefire along the 38th parallel. But General MacArthur isn't content with a ceasefire. That's why he's ordering his troops in the South to invade the North."

We put our clubs into the back seat of our little Opal Cabriolet sports car, and Dad tuned into the German Blaupunkt short wave radio. Often on our clear Sunday morning outings, we were able to pick up the previous evening's news from

Salinas, California. Today was no different, except for the breaking news. The newscaster reported that President Truman had relieved General MacArthur of his command and ordered him to return to the States.

As the newscaster continued his report, Dad spun the car around and told me we were driving to the Whitneys'. Obviously upset by the radio news, Dad wanted to learn what General Whitney knew. Major General Courtney Whitney not only served as the senior officer on General MacArthur's staff, but he and Mrs. Whitney were also godparents to my new baby sister, Sarah Elizabeth. When we reached the Whitney house, Dad left me in the car as he went inside to talk to the general. After a few minutes, the general came out the front door, waved to me, then left for the Embassy to confer with General MacArthur. Dad and I drove home.

It was Wednesday, April 11, 1951. General MacArthur had not yet received official communication from the States. The news had only been communicated to him by the reports of those who had heard the stateside news broadcast. I learned later that General MacArthur showed no emotion when told. He turned calming to Mrs. MacArthur and said, "Jeannie, we're going home at last."

My personal response to the news came the next morning when I went to school and turned the American flag upside down before lowering it to half-staff. My father's rank and persuasion were all that kept me from being expelled for what I considered merely an act of loyalty.

The Lifelong Misfit

As my high school years drew to a close, I did not want to return to that faraway place my parents called "home." I could hardly remember Chicago, my birthplace, or any of the many places we had lived before moving to Japan. I considered Tokyo "home." Home: where my friends lived. Home: where I had gone to high school. Mother and Dad kept reminding me that the United States was my "real home." Maybe their home, but not home to me!

My parents won the final decision of where I would attend college. And so I returned "home" and started college at Jackson College for Women, the women's college of Tufts University in Medford, a suburb of Boston, Massachusetts. What a huge culture shock! I walked across Cambridge Square, turning my head whenever I heard English spoken. In Tokyo I only heard English at home or in school – never on the street. It took a long time and some confusion for me to get used to hearing English constantly being spoken by everyone around me.

The clothes my classmates wore provided another culture shock. I hadn't even unpacked completely when my roommate looked at the clothes laid out on my bed and proclaimed them "so out of date." I acquired my college wardrobe from pictures in Seventeen Magazine, which my dressmaker then carefully reproduced. I assumed clothes in a current magazine depicted the latest styles - what everyone wore back "home." But Seventeen Magazine apparently didn't represent Boston college apparel. My roommate carted me off to a store called Filene's Basement. She picked out apparel more suitable – Bermuda shorts, long socks, and saddle shoes. I went along with her. I desperately wanted to look like everyone else, even if I didn't feel like everyone else. The trip to Filene's Basement reinforced my growing fears: I could never belong.

I'm not sure why I didn't want my new college friends to know where I went to high school. They might think me weird, or worse, "too cool" for them, having lived abroad. Being "cool" ran the risk of being different. And being different meant not belonging. So when someone detected my non-Bostonian accent and asked me where I came from, I responded that I hailed from the Midwest, my birthplace and where my parents grew up.

One evening, the girls on my dorm floor decided to boycott the cafeteria and walk down to Ball Square for supper. I reluctantly accepted their invitation to join them, still intent on trying to fit in and be like everyone else. Maybe the invitation meant I could be accepted after all.

The first warning came when my dormitory mates chose a Japanese restaurant for dinner. Had I known the restaurant they planned to choose, I would have declined their invitation. Now it was too late. We walked in the door and the hostess greeted us in Japanese. I caught myself in time from replying. I laughed along with the others as my roommate tried to imitate her greeting and funny accent. But the knot in my stomach traveled upward toward my throat.

Our waiter passed out menus. I carefully focused my eyes on the English side of the menu – occasionally trying to glance surreptitiously at the Japanese side to see what the dishes might actually be. The waiter took our orders. I made sure to order something that one of the other girls had already ordered so that I could repeat her Americanized pronunciation.

As we waited for our entrees to arrive, my new friends talked about their classes, laughed about the biology professor who always wore the same corduroy sports coat. We admitted jokingly which male classmate we most wanted for a lab partner. Our food arrived. Conversation stopped as each of my friends tasted their food and sampled each other's selections. One of the girls stared at me, exclaiming, "Look at how she holds her chopsticks." She turned to me: "Where in the world did you learn to use chopsticks like that? You'd think you were Japanese!" What could I say? The evening was ruined. So were my expectations. Could I ever belong in this place my parents called "home?"

The Easter Message

Growing up, Easter morning began with a knock on my bedroom door and Dad's *basso profundo* voice announcing loudly, "Alleluia! He is risen!" Not until I replied, "The Lord is risen indeed. Alleluia!" did Dad then move on to his next child's bedroom door, where he repeated his wake-up greeting.

My first year back in the United States at Tufts brought a lonely spring break. Spring break didn't coincide with Easter, and my family lived much too far away for me to travel home for the holiday. That first Easter morning, I could only think about how much I missed my family as I headed for the cafeteria for breakfast and then down the hill to church. By myself. All alone.

Several hours later, as I trudged up the hill to return to my dormitory, I saw our housemother. She called to me, waving an envelope in her hand. As I approached the front door, she greeted me, "You have a telegram from home, my dear." With fear and trembling I tore open the Western Union envelope. The message read: "Alleluia he is risen STOP." I ran down the hall to the pay phone on the wall. A telephone directory dangled from the phone box. I tore through the yellow pages until I found the address of the nearest Western Union office. Running down the hill and into the Square, I could hardly wait to send my reply. "The Lord is risen indeed Alleluia STOP."

Many Easter mornings have come and gone. Western Union has been replaced by email and instant messaging. Our family is scattered all over the globe, and I have become the matriarch of our family. The ritual is now up to me.

It is Easter morning. I am sitting at my desk. Laptop open. I send the message

"Alleluia. He is risen" to my sisters and my brother; next to my sons; then to my grandchildren one by one. I wait with joyous anticipation. The laptop begins to beep. One reply. And then another. And another…

Beep. "The Lord is risen indeed. Alleluia." Beep. "The Lord is risen indeed. Alleluia." Beep. Beep. Beep.

Part 3

Marriage,
Motherhood,
Mathematician
1955-1984

A Look in the Mirror

If I could have thought of a response, I would have answered his onslaught with my own words, but this sudden barrage left me speechless. For twelve years I had assumed our marriage was near perfect. We had created four beautiful young human beings, whom I thought we both adored – one of a number of assumptions I had made about his feelings toward our children, toward me, and now toward our marriage. Suddenly, my identity as a wife and mother was shattered. How could I have been so mistaken about myself and my role in life?

We left the boys with a babysitter and strolled down to the beach for what I thought to be a romantic hour together. Instead, I sat with toes wiggling in the sand, bombarded with more emotion from my husband than I had ever experienced. But this emotional outburst was far from the loving words and feelings I had expected. Anger spurted out of his every pore. His words bombarded me, striking me with my failures, transgressions, and shortcomings. I suddenly saw myself through my beloved's eyes as unattractive, unappealing, uncaring, and unsuccessful in every aspect as a wife and mother. In a few short minutes, he completely destroyed my identity: I became unloved, unwanted - a total failure.

It took me years of failed relationships, years of tears and self-recrimination, years of therapy to look back on that night on the beach with less jaundiced understanding. I was not mistaken about myself. I was not the miserable failure after all. The sand and a crestfallen wife were only mirrors of what he had been actually shouting about himself. And now, all these years later, I wonder how many failures, how many misunderstandings, how many broken relationships are not really about the other person at all – but only a reflection of what might better be addressed by looking in the mirror.

.

When in Rome. . .

My brother-in-law, first and foremost a military man, ran his home like a barracks and his family like a platoon. Dinner time at his house began with a formal military inspection. My sons, referred to as "the troops" by their Uncle Hal, scrubbed their hands and faces until their cheeks became pink. They carefully tucked in their shirttails, ran a brush through their hair even when they had a buzz cut, then lined up standing at attention, looking straight ahead. They extended their arms to have hands and nails inspected. Only after passing inspection did Uncle Hal give permission for the boys to march single file into the dining room and stand at attention behind their chairs until the adults sat down.

Aunt Emmy placed serving dishes at the head of the table – Uncle Hal's command post. He served the adults first, inquiring about dishes and quantities desired. Not so with the boys. He determined what and how much to place on each boy's plate. They had to eat what they had been served – no questions asked, no dismayed looks, no declining any of his vegetables. If a boy cleaned his plate, he could request a second helping. No dessert if Uncle Hal detected even a hint of untouched food. A clean plate carried an immediate reward: a scrumptious piece of homemade pie topped with ice cream.

But the real reward awaited dinner's end: a trip to the basement. Lionel train tracks covered a large table, replete with a miniature village, trains, and switches to produce lights, whistles, and control the trains along the tracks. Each visit Uncle Hal picked one boy to sit on the special bench, don a trainmaster's cap, and run the trains. The boys considered being chosen as trainmaster equivalent to receiving the Medal of Honor.

At our home, there were no rewards for a clean plate and no special treat awaiting the meal's end. One particular evening, one of my sons dashed in from playing outdoors, sat down, and reached for the bowl of potatoes. He didn't wait for me to sit down or plates to be served: a bit too casual even for our household. To make matters worse, his hands and face were filthy. I reacted immediately: "Go wash your hands." He looked at me in wide-eyed astonishment. "Why?" he asked. "We're not at Uncle Hal's house."

Dinner inspection at Uncle Hal's house had become a ritual in which my sons played soldier. My children accepted washing hands before sitting down at the dinner table as a cultural expectation of being at Uncle Hal's, completely divorced from cleanliness as a prerequisite for coming to the dinner table. Apparently, my sons assumed that dinner time at home was a different culture.

I have struggled most of my life with cultural adaptation. Many of my values and habits were formed in the Japanese culture in which I grew up. But even while still living in Japan, my parents' midwestern upbringing also subjected me to a rather typical American way of life. I quite literally straddled two cultures as a teenager. Returning to the United States to attend college immersed me in the culture of my parents, but I often lapsed into cultural responses formed by my "adopted" Japanese homeland. As I struggled to belong, with one foot in each of two cultures, my sons taught me an important lesson about adjusting to expectations and situations of more than one culture. Some might describe differing cultural expectations as "when in Rome..." My boys called it simply "when at Uncle Hal's..."

Kalamazoo Snowstorm

I gazed out the window while my students copied the formula I had written on the blackboard. The snow fell steadily. Not unusual for Kalamazoo at this time of year, but when the snow shifted from flakes to white sheets, I suddenly became more concerned about my children than my students. I faced the classroom: "That seems like a good place to stop for the day. We'll pick up another example of the distributive law tomorrow. In the meantime, perhaps you can think of several more examples of the tau function."

I gathered up my papers quickly and headed to the Teaching Assistants' office for my coat and boots. The snow came at me sideways as I maneuvered the little VW station wagon out of the parking lot and headed toward home. Three miles. Could I make it? The snow hadn't been falling long enough for the city snowplows to begin clearing the roadway. I crossed the expressway and headed into Portage, the suburban community where the boys and I lived. The snow got thicker and deeper. Two miles to go. An abandoned car blocked part of the roadway. I maneuvered around it, worried now about the boys: Had their classes been dismissed? How could they get home? Would the school try to bus the children home? Will and Charlie rode the middle school bus, but Barry and Jamie usually walked to their elementary school.

I caught a glimpse of Barry trudging along the roadway. I honked and skidded to a stop to gather up my youngest son. I pulled him into the car.

"Have you seen Jamie?"

"No, but the whole school got let out. The teacher told us to call our parents, but I knew you were teaching, so I started to walk home. No clue about Jamie. I'm freezing."

"Take your gloves off and rub your hands together. They'll warm up and we'll be home soon. Keep your eyes on the lookout for your brothers."

One mile. Where were the other boys? We crossed the middle school's street. Where were Will and Charlie? Could they have made it home already? I caught sight of two boys in the street ahead of me, throwing snowballs at each other -- Jamie and the boy who lived across the street. I honked. The boys waved. I motioned to them as the car skidded into the ditch.

Jamie tried to shovel the snow away from the back tires – between throwing snowballs. The other boys got in front, trying to push the car backwards as I rocked the car back and forth. The car skidded further and further into the snow.

I began to shiver. We were all getting colder and colder. I took the red bandana which we kept in the glove compartment and tied it around the antenna – a signal to the snowplow of a car in the snowbank. It was getting hard to see across the street. Holding hands, we trudged through the deepening snow toward home. It took us almost another hour to go those last couple of blocks. Soon a whiteout would cause our houses to disappear. Where were Will and Charlie? How could I even try to go looking for them? How could I get help to locate my oldest sons? I blinked away tears. I couldn't let myself cry in front of my children.

As we got to the end of the driveway leading to our house, the next-door neighbor rushed out of her kitchen door and began to wave at us. She shouted that her husband had picked up the twins. They were in her kitchen eating cookies and drinking milk. We were home; all four boys accounted for. Together. Safe. I sighed with huge relief.

After warm baths, the boys watched TV while I fixed dinner. What a relief that I'd done grocery shopping on Tuesday. We weren't going anywhere soon. At least we had plenty of food.

The boys laughed as they called to me: "Mom, you have to come look out the window." A neighbor had attached a pair of skis to the wheels of a wagon, as he maneuvered through the snow on snowshoes. Did he need food? Should I offer him some of our canned goods? I opened the front door a crack to call out to him, but he was already out of sight. Over an hour later, the boys spotted him returning – a case of beer showing through the slats of the wagon. The boys got a bit of a laugh about "essential supplies."

Three days later, the neighbors, my boys, and I donned snow boots, hats, and gloves and ventured out in search of our cars. As we spotted the antenna of each car along the roadway, we shoveled; we pushed; we laid cardboard under back tires. One by one, with community effort, we retrieved all our abandoned cars.

The boys remember getting an extra mid-winter break and watching movies and eating popcorn; I remember how frightened I had been for my children's safety. that we had plenty of food and didn't lose power; the people of Kalamazoo remember "the great snowfall of 1967."

My Home Sweet Home

When I returned from Japan to the United States to attend college, I felt confused and totally out of place in the land of my birth. I had never watched TV. My clothes bore no resemblance to the styles my new friends were wearing. My experiences living abroad were so essentially different from my classmates who lived their entire lives in one New England community. My classmates' views of the world seemed near-sighted. A total culture shock. Despite my Chicago birth, I felt like an expat or a resident alien. I struggled with accepting and embracing America as "home" for almost two decades.

Then along came the summer of 1976. By this time, I was a college professor spending summers doing fire behavior research at

Glacier National Park. Between hours counting lodgepole pine trees in the park and even longer hours creating computer models of what happened to the forests when lightning struck, I did a lot of hiking and backpacking.

I hiked with friends who were forest rangers most weekends. One of my hiking buddies suggested that we make a special hike over the Fourth of July to commemorate the 200th anniversary of our nation's independence. We hitchhiked along Going-To-The-Sun Road from our campsites in West Glacier to the northeastern edge of the park. We began our hike by crossing the border to Watertown Lakes in Alberta, Canada, then hiking back to the U.S. side of the Rockies through Ptarmigan Pass. On July 3rd we reached the summit, where we set up camp for the night.

At dawn on the Fourth of July, we stood together at the top of the pass to watch the sunrise. Our far-reaching view encompassed both sides of the Rockies: The United States and Canada. The magnificence of dense pine forests interspersed with meadows interspersed with small ponds. The watersheds that comprise the continental Divide.

A bald eagle soared overhead as a member of our group began to sing "God bless America, land that I love…" And at that moment on the top of Ptarmigan Pass, the country of my birth finally became "my home sweet home."

The Hike I Didn't Take

One of the great joys of spending summers at Glacier National Park was doing research on forest ecosystems. As part of a small consulting company, I helped develop models to predict the spread and changes in forests when lightning strikes. But neither the research nor the publications nor even the scholarly recognition of the publications made summers at Glacier so special. My greatest enjoyment came from the thrill and beauty of hiking many of the challenging trails that zigzag through the million acres that compose the park.

Glacier National Park has always been home to both black and grizzly bears. From my first hike in the 1970s, I learned to be on the lookout for bears. We attached cowbells to our backpacks to announce our presence and to scare off all wildlife. Although bears can climb trees, their sense of sight and smell usually prevents them from following a human being up a tree. Today, hikers are encouraged to stand their ground, looking a bear straight in the eye, but when I began hiking, tree climbing constituted our first defense.

My friends and I took only freeze-dried food on hikes and buried all our garbage. We took extensive hygiene precautions to prevent bears from detecting human smells: washing our bodies thoroughly at day's end and never wearing perfume or deodorant when hiking. We even hung our clothes and shoes (that might smell of human perspiration) on branches some distance from our tent.

Most often, I hiked with two women forest rangers who were in their early thirties, experienced campers and trained botanists. They taught me, a forty-something-year old mathematician, to identify the flora and fauna of the park. Every hike with them created a learning experience.

At the end of August, one of the "gals," as they were called by their male colleagues, approached me: "Why don't you join us on our Labor Day Weekend adventure?"

The other piped up: "We're thinking about hiking up to Dawson Pass. We'll camp and hike the whole Labor Day weekend."

"We'll hike the entire 17-mile Ptarmigan Loop. It'll be a challenge; a great all-girls' hiking trip," the first gal added.

"Come with us," they both urged me.

Sorely tempted, *but.* . .with plans that fall to teach a new upper-level math course in Combinatorics for senior majors and first year graduate students at Rockford College, I needed time to get home before the Labor Day weekend to get prepared. I declined the hiking invitation. My hiking buddies urged me to reconsider. And I was so tempted.

"I'd love to, but I really can't."

Back and forth – urging and declining. In the end, my better judgment prevailed, and I headed home to Rockford.

I sat at the dining room table, surrounded by textbooks, references, lecture notes, citations, - all staring up at me as I sat chewing on the end of my pencil. It always took a few days to adjust to being home after a summer in Glacier, and my mind kept wandering. I knew I had to get these lectures written, or I'd be playing catch up all semester. But I kept thinking about Dawson pass and seeing Bighorn Basin at sunrise. The phone rang. I picked up the receiver. Silence at the end of the line. Finally, my friend, the Dawson Pass park ranger, spoke softly, "Meredith, it's Pete."

"Oh, Pete. Did you hear from the gals? How did the hike go? I still wish I'd been able to join them."

Pete sounded as if he might be choking. "It's about the hike … two bears . . . the girls…both of them."

I took a deep breath. Choking back his sobs, he told me, "They were camping overnight at the Two Medicine Campground…I'm not sure why…guess they wanted to reach Dawson Pass at sunrise. I was on duty at the ranger station when I received the call. The camper who called me said one of the gals had tried to climb a nearby tree, but the first bear grabbed her by the leg and wrestled her to the ground. The second bear - maybe the first bear's cub - attacked the other gal as she tried to come to her friend's rescue. The gals were both badly mauled by the time I got there. We took them by helicopter to the hospital in Missoula. None of us can believe it . . . both of them. . . they were always so careful . . . I just didn't get there in time . . ."

After finally hanging up the phone, I sat in stunned silence. I began to cry. How could that have happened? My mind raced from one what-if to another: what if I had decided to stay and hike that weekend? What if I had been with them when the bears attacked? What if I had been attacked? What if. . .?

Even today, when I think of my years of hiking in Glacier National Park - the spectacular sunrises, the glacier lakes, the dense forests - my thoughts inevitably return to my hiking companions and the hike I didn't take.

*L*ook *B*efore you *S*wat

Even as a child, Charlie had a love for cars, and his mechanical skills were evident long before he became a professional. During high school, he often brought home vehicles in need of a new engine or other major restoration. During his junior year, he acquired a 1965 Econoline van, which he decided would make a great family camper. He remedied the van's mechanical challenges first, then proceeded to outfit the interior. He installed a sink and Coleman propane stove to create a makeshift kitchen. He built cabinets along one wall and hooks for a shovel, fly swatter, and broom. The second seat provided space for three passengers and a bed at night.

Charlie hadn't finished converting the van, but as he was working part time, he couldn't join us for the weekend camping trip. I prevailed upon him to let me take his

younger brothers for a weekend camping
test run. Barry and Jamie each tucked a
beer crate of clothes and games onto the
shelves behind the rear seat. They loaded
food, sleeping bags, a pup tent, barbecue
tools, a shovel, and fly swatter – my
favorite discipline threat to both flies and
boys.

Off we went to Naperville to pick up
my nephew, Randy, before heading to the
Ottawa National Forest in northern
Wisconsin. The cousins were close in age
and loved to camp, swim, fish, and enjoy
summer together. The maiden voyage for
the family's new camper van. The promise
of a fun weekend for the cousins.

We found a campsite in the park, close
to the restrooms and the lake. The boys
started grabbing swimming suits out of
their crates, but I insisted: First things first.
The boys gathered wood for a fire pit, put
up their pup tent. Finishing their tasks
quickly, they ducked into the tent, pulled
on bathing suits and ran to the lake. I

watched them from our campsite. Splashing. Shouting "Look!" as they showed me their latest swimming stunt. Time to call them back to the campsite before dark to help make spaghetti – their supper choice. The boys gathered twigs. After much arguing about whether kindling needed to form a pyramid or a teepee, they got a fire started. I took a large pan from the cupboard in the van and began to cook noodles over the fire. One of the boys put the Prego sauce in a small pan and lit the stove in the camper while I tossed lettuce and tomatoes into a salad.

As the sun began to set, a breeze came up and we all changed into long pants and sweatshirts. We sat on the logs around the campfire to keep warm. The salad went largely untouched, but the boys ate several helpings of rolls and spaghetti. Dinner ended with the traditional s'mores: marshmallows eaten between graham crackers and melted pieces of chocolate.

The boys retrieved sticks from hooks in the camper, which they'd carved during a previous trip, and toasted marshmallows over the campfire. Time for the usual contest to determine who made the best-looking s'mores sandwich.

Time to clean up. The boys carted leftovers into the camper icebox as I washed the pans in the sink, then placed them to dry on the logs near the fire. Time for bed. The boys crawled into their sleeping bags, but I could see lights illuminating the pup tent. Probably trying to read comic books by flashlight. Half an hour later I declared, "Lights out, boys," retreated to the van, closed the door, stretched out on the backseat/bed and called it a night. Or so I hoped. Camping with three boys exhausted me, but it also lifted my spirits, and I laughed quietly as I listened in on their conversations. Randy called to me, "Aunt Meredith, Barry's farting." Laughter from the boys. I had no intention of mediating a gas passing contest. More laughter as I told the boys, "Time to knock it off. Go to sleep."

I drifted off to sleep myself. The sound of the van's back door awakened me. The icebox door creaked as the boys retrieved leftovers. I watched them stoke the coals, set a pan on the fire and prepare a second meal. I got out of my van bed, breathing deeply to maintain my patience and control my irritation as I leaned out the van door and said, "Boys. This is the last time I'm telling you. Clean up your mess and get back to bed before I have to resort to something stronger than words." I retreated to the camper and back to bed. I drifted back to sleep, still listening to the boys giggling and rattling pans.

I jumped awake to more rustling sounds by the campfire. Were the boys eating again? No more patience. I grabbed the fly swatter off its hook in the camper, slipped into my shoes, and headed for the campfire. I began to swat the figure over the campfire again and again, shouting, "I told you to go to bed!" Randy heard my angry voice and stuck his head out the pup tent. Astonished, he hollered to his cousins: "Hey, guys, you've got to see this! Your mother is spanking a bear."

Hard to be a Woman

I hadn't thought much about the role of women or discrimination, growing up in Japan. My baby brother definitely occupied the place of honor among the servants – and maybe even with my parents – but I attributed his favoritism to his being the baby – not his being the boy in the family. I even excused the frustration of not being able to acolyte at church services or becoming a priest when I grew up to ancient Catholic custom – not gender discrimination. I married and bore children right out of college – traditional roles for a woman of my generation. But now I found myself in an uncomfortable role – a single woman in a society that expected me to be happily married. Facing the necessity of feeding my children – a role typically relegated to the man in the family.

I slit open the envelope from the University of Michigan. Another graduate school application rejected. Twelve years earlier those same colleges had offered me a fellowship, but apparently a thirty-two-year-old woman with young children presented a risk they weren't willing to take. Did they think my brain had atrophied? Several more rejections, then Western Michigan University took a chance, and I enrolled in their M.A. degree program in Mathematics. The goal – a teaching credential and the ability to support my family. Mathematicians – male and female – could earn a living. An actuary friend of Dad's offered me a job at his insurance company. But I hoped to teach. I didn't want only to feed my young boys. I wanted summers to parent them with camping trips and fun adventures. I wanted to be the wage earner, yet still be their mother.

Difficult the return to the classroom after twelve years away from mathematics.

Three rounds of measles and a boy's tonsillectomy complicated life. One professor assumed I would babysit his children – free. That wasn't the only assumption he made. I declined his advances. It cost me an A in his class – and an unfairly rough time when orals came around. The price of being a woman – especially a single woman – in a predominantly male field. But, specifically, the only woman in that professor's class.

Other impediments. Other experiences of being a single woman kept hitting me in the face. Shell Oil Company invited all graduate teaching assistants to apply for their credit card. My colleagues and I filled out the applications and waited expectantly. The male teaching assistants began receiving their cards. The women waited. My rejection letter explained that my teaching assistant's stipend fell below their income minimums. Apparently, I needed the supplementary income of a "working wife." Strange. A number of the men who received their Shell credit cards didn't have working wives.

A local car dealership offered graduate students an opportunity to trade in older vehicles, with no down payment and low interest until graduation. I visited the dealership. The salesman ignored me. Didn't he want me to buy a new car? I finally got his attention. He didn't show me any new cars. He suggested I let my husband pick out the new car. I should have known better.

The washing machine died. Bill and I had opened a Sears account shortly after we married to buy that first washer and dryer when the twins were born. After four children and years of cloth diapers, it was time for a trade-in. I went to the Sears store in Kalamazoo, assuming I still had a Sears account. The salesman assured me the account could be reactivated. Then he told me I needed my "husband's signature" to use it. I tried to open a new account in my own name. That brought on a demeaning laugh. Apparently, out of the question for a woman to have her own account. Buying a new washing machine remained also out of the question until Dad cosigned a bank loan. One male signature swapped for another. At least the children and I could now have clean clothes.

But I did have a job. Nearby Kalamazoo College needed a math instructor for one year to replace a faculty member on sabbatical. I loved teaching. I loved teaching college students. The year ended much too soon. Then back on the job market.

I interviewed at the national meetings of mathematicians. Much to my surprise and relief, offers came in. University of Akron. Bemidji State University. Indiana University of Pennsylvania. Not exactly the small liberal arts college in Michigan I hoped for. I could be an "instructor" with possibility for promotion and tenure track after a year. No moving expenses. No guarantee beyond the first year. Not exactly what this mother of four young sons had toiled and sweated for the past three years. Then Beloit College in Wisconsin posted a job opening. I got an interview. The interview seemed to go great. But they did not offer me a job–I had no Ph.D. and concentration in the wrong area of mathematics. But the chair of the math department passed on my name to the department chair at Rockford College across the border in Illinois. I interviewed. I received an offer. A great offer: Assistant Professorship with a tenure track appointment. The dream job – but not in Michigan where I had envisioned living and remaining close to family.

The college helped me find a house to rent. A former trustee's widow, not yet ready to sell. We met. She welcomed me warmly and seemed genuinely delighted for her house to be occupied by a faculty family. What a relief to find a four-bedroom house I could afford. I returned to her house to sign the lease. She looked surprised. "Where is Professor Potter? I'll need him to sign the lease."

"I thought you realized when we were introduced that I'm Professor Potter."

Her demeanor changed. She became abrupt. "I'm so sorry, but I couldn't possibly rent to a single woman with children."

No amount of pleading, even from the College administration, could change her mind. I felt completely helpless - trapped by society's discrimination against women. I had overcome what seemed like insurmountable odds, only to face what seemed like another impossible obstacle. How could I accept a teaching position if I couldn't find a home for my family? Would I have to decline the position? Once again, panic set in. How could I support my family? Rockford College stepped up. They found a realtor to help me purchase a home. Not even an assistant professor's salary kept this single woman from being too big a loan risk. The college co-signed that first mortgage!

I had faced discrimination. Doors had slammed in my face. I was harassed. But in spite of everything, my career took off. I became the founding chair of a new department: Computer Science. My research in environmental modeling of forest ecosystems produced publication after publication. Promotion after promotion. Even a number of lucrative consulting opportunities. A full professorship and tenure. I watched the world's opportunities for women change steadily. Even the Episcopal Church got on board: women could now become priests. Maybe one day.

That day arrived in the spring of 1982. I became an empty nester. I had job security. A growing professional reputation. A professorship with tenure, doubling my teaching salary by consulting. I had made it in spite of every obstacle. And I chose to give up everything

I had accomplished. I could now realize the dream of my youth that afternoon on a hillside in Hokkaido – the yearning and calling to be a priest. I resigned from my professorship. I published my last research paper. I traveled to Australia for my last consulting trip. I enrolled in seminary to become a priest.

This second adventure of graduate school proved to be markedly different from the first. At seminary where women and men were treated equally, I even achieved the doctorate that had once been beyond my reach.

Now, I look back on almost four decades of service to the Lord. Not only my life, but the lives and expectations for women in our society continue to change. Women demand and achieve so many more opportunities. Women now charge their way into almost every profession. Equal opportunity and equal treatment – once unmet demands– are now the law. Professions can no longer advertise male only. Women now demand equal pay for equal work. Today women seldom tolerate harassment and discrimination in silence. We demand respect for our achievements and for our bodies. During my lifetime, women forced open doors that society once slammed in our faces. We can get credit cards and mortgages. The obstacles, the challenges, the unfairness I faced were all worth it if my granddaughters and great-granddaughters never have to experience in their lives how hard it was to be a woman.

Professor Meredith Potter

Part 4

A Priest Forever

1985-

The Red MG

My sophomore year in high school, I fell in love. Every weekend I stood at the window and watched for his car to roar into the driveway. And when I caught a glimpse of my love approaching, my heart began to pound. Ned and I were going steady. Only I didn't love Ned. I loved his sports car! I tutored Ned in geometry and trig; he introduced me to opera and sports cars. And of all the sports cars I learned to identify, my heart leapt for that one particular car: an MG. Ned and I graduated from high school and went our separate ways, but I never forgot my first love, and whenever I saw an MG on the highway, I thought to myself, "Someday, I'm going to own a red MG."

As the years went by, I transported my growing family in station wagons. But I must have instilled my love for sports cars in my sons, for they often pointed to a fancy sports car on the highway, "Now there's a car for you, Mom." Then came the opportunity. My son Charlie, now grown and serving in the army in California, called me to say a fellow soldier had orders for overseas and had to sell his 1974 MGB. I flew to California. At long last I had the car of my dreams; I owned my very own red MG.

The car helped me create a whole new persona. I felt attractive and dashing and eccentric whenever I stepped into my MG. I enjoyed being recognized and admired, as I drove the only red MG in Rockford, Illinois. I could always count on the cares of the world "blowing away" as I raced through the countryside with the top down. I owned the car of my dreams. It never occurred to me that the car might own me.

One day after my children had left the nest, I sold my house, left Rockford and my

successful academic career. I left most of my
familiar and comfortable life behind. I moved
to nearby Evanston to attend seminary. The
red MG went with me. I rationalized: after all,
I surely needed a car to get to my internship
church on Sundays. I continued to tell myself:
the car gets good mileage and it's already paid
for!

In my second year in seminary during a
New Testament class we began to discuss one
of Jesus' parables about a rich young man,
who asked the "good rabbi" how he could win
the greatest prize of all: eternal life. My
classmates all agreed the young man was what
the world called "a real winner." He was rich,
intelligent,   successful   (and   probably
handsome, we conjectured) and he wanted to
win at being a good Jew. We all laughed when
a classmate remarked that Jesus invited this
"winner" to become a loser. Our laughter
became   more   poignant   when   someone
suggested that thankfully none of us had to
face the rich young man's dilemma. We had all
become losers when we came to seminary. We

had lost our jobs and professions; we had given up being near family, familiar and comfortable surroundings; we had lost our financial security. As the discussion of the rich young man continued, and more of my classmates began to share their stories of all they'd given up and how they had become "losers," I became more and more uncomfortable. I hadn't given up anything that really mattered to me. I still had my most prized possession; I still had my red MG.

As seminary days went on, I couldn't get the story of the rich young man out of my mind. I reflected on his unwillingness to give up his possessions. I couldn't get my red MG out of my mind. I began to wonder whether I would be willing to give it up. And then something quite unexpected happened. In spite of careful planning, I ran out of money. A long-time admirer of my car came to my rescue. The next time he asked me how much I wanted for my car, I blurted out the calculated amount I needed to finish seminary.

Immediately, he wrote me a check and drove away in my beloved red MG.

I went back to my room and cried. My tears were not tears of grief for the loss of what had been so dear to me; my tears were not even tears of relief that my financial problem had been solved. My tears came from the recognition that I could have been that rich young man, except that now, by God's grace, my story had the possibility of a different ending. I had not remained possessed by my most prized possession.

In recent years, I have been driving a white hybrid Honda CRZ. Honda quit producing the model shortly after I purchased it, because the company couldn't seem to market "a little old lady's sports car." This little old lady loves racing down River Road with its twists and turns, managing to control the turns with the accelerator and not the brakes. Sometimes, I even allow my imagination to take over and pretend that my white Honda is the red MG of my youth.

Don't Make the Pastor Cry

"Peace at any price." Mother's maxim from my childhood still rings in my ears whenever I find myself approaching a conflict. As a youngster frustrated to tears by my younger sister, I begged by mother, "She's lying as usual; make her tell me the truth!" But the argument always concluded with Mother's words. Mother made it clear. The argument was over.

"Pass it by in silence," demanded Mother, declaring her second maxim, her way of addressing and resolving every argument with my sister, every misunderstanding, every conflict. Considering how arguments were resolved not only in my family, but in the Japanese culture in which I had been raised, it's no wonder Mother's maxims dictated how I approached conflict even as an adult.

While attending a weekend conflict management workshop as a new priest, the leader asked me to summarize in only one sentence my personal conflict resolution style. Which maxim to choose? Which of Mother's words best described my own stance on life? Chewing my pencil, I realized my life – my mother's influence coupled with Asian culture in which I had been raised - had given birth to my own maxim: "Sip tea and flee." This maxim had defined my marriage and its breakup, my years of navigating the politics of academia. Had it not been for a near disaster, "sip tea and flee" might well have come to define my years of ministry.

The vestry meeting in the Korean congregation began quite normally. Reports were interrupted only when I, their newly assigned vicar, asked for a translation. And then it happened! The treasurer introduced his report. Not five words into the expense summary, the senior warden cut him off: "Did you pay the bill for the new windowsills?" Another vestry member jumped to his feet: "That better not have been paid. The repairman charged entirely too much. I could have repaired it myself." Voices grew louder as one by one everyone began shouting opinions. My fluency in Japanese didn't help me understand the colloquial Korean idioms that were flying back and forth.

I was flabbergasted to hear men shouting at each other. My father never raised his voice; the Japanese businessmen who often frequented our home were controlled, manipulative, but always softspoken. These vestry members were shouting at each other – and over a carpenter's bill, for god's sake! I shouted, "Stop," but the men's shouting muted my attempts to gain control. The vestry obviously wouldn't pass the matter by in silence.

The treasurer stood up. He threw his report at the senior warden. A fleeting moment of silence. At that moment when I thought I could now take control, the senior warden also stood. He raised both hands stiffly in front of him and stepped toward the treasurer. He gave the treasurer a shove. The treasurer responded by punching his adversary in the nose. Everyone began to shout and shove. An outright brawl in the making.

I collapsed into tears. I had no experience dealing with Korean men. My still rudimentary language skills left me helpless. How would I ever lead this congregation? I sobbed in utter despair; as I hiccupped, every vestry member stared at me in astonished silence. I had regained control; the argument concluded. I had given birth to a new maxim: "Don't make the pastor cry."

Encounter with a Demon

In the middle of the day in the middle of the week, I sat in my office at St. Richard's Episcopal Church in Chicago. The Korean congregation I served had outgrown the little church in Albany Park. We were now renting space at St. Richard's in Edgebrook, located on busy Devon Avenue, but I felt comfortable being in the church alone during the day. I heard the church door open and stepped out of my office, fully expecting to see Fr. Kurt Olson, rector of St. Richard's, or one of the altar guild members. Instead, I encountered a well-dressed middle aged Caucasian woman walking toward Fr. Olson's office.

"I'm Mother Potter, the vicar of St. Mary's Korean congregation. Fr. Olson isn't here right now, can I assist you?"

"I'm curious about the church. I'm not quite sure I know what Episcopal means." She sounded curious and yet a bit anxious as she continued down the hall.

"Well, let me try to explain. The Episcopal Church had its origins in England as part of the universal Catholic Church. But in the 16th century, when ..."

The woman's eyes began to glaze over, and I thought I had either bored her or I had misunderstood her question. Then she began to drool. She opened her mouth, and a large masculine voice began to shout horrible, vulgar words - blasphemous phrases about God and Jesus and the Church. As I stood horror-stricken, the woman sank to her knees, then fell to the floor. The shouts from her mouth continued as I stood there, suddenly horrified and terrified. Then without any conscious thought, I heard myself shout back at the voice, "IN THE NAME OF JESUS CHRIST, STOP!"

Immediate silence. The woman stood up, brushed off her skirt, and said to me in her own, quite normal voice, "It's been lovely meeting you. I hope to see you again soon." She turned, and before I could reply, she walked out the door. I watched her amble down the street, too paralyzed even to call after her.

I returned to my office and sat down, taking deep breaths, until my heartbeat quit pounding in my chest, and my breathing began to return to normal. What now? What could I do? Such an encounter remained well outside the realm of "normal parish ministry." What had just happened fell beyond my training; it also fell beyond the scope of my ministry. I blew my nose, picked up the phone, and called the Diocesan Center.

"May I speak to Bishop Griswold. It's Meredith Potter, and I think it's an emergency." The receptionist replied, "One moment, please." A long silence. Then I heard the familiar Pennsylvania twang of the bishop: "Good afternoon, Meredith. How are you? How are those wonderful Korean people of yours? I understand you're doing great things since moving to St. Richard's."

Bishop Griswold had not only ordained me to the priesthood several years earlier, he had become my mentor and my friend; but today, more importantly, my "boss." I began to cry as I described my encounter with the woman. The bishop didn't interrupt me.

"… and then she walked out the door."

Silence at the other end of the phone. Then the bishop said, "Meredith, are you alright? Is Kurt (Fr. Olson) there with you? Do I need to send someone to St. Richard's?"

"No, I'm alone, and I guess I'm alright. What should I have done? Am I in trouble?"

Gently, the bishop reminded me that the Holy Spirit enables ordained priests to carry out the ministry of healing the sick, restoring the disenfranchised, offering Jesus' forgiveness of sin, proclaiming the Good News of Salvation. "But," he continued, "Jesus did one thing that the church has been cautious about, namely, casting out demons. It's not that the church doesn't recognize evil, but rather that evil can be quite dangerous. That's why in every diocese, exorcism - the casting out of demons - is restricted to a designated priest who is specially trained. That's why you have been instructed to consult with me if you suspect demonic activity, and to ask for the designated priest to deal with any such problem."

"Did I cast out a demon? How could I have called you first?" I repeated my concern: "Am I in trouble?"

"Well, Meredith. It certainly sounds as if you cast out a demon. But obviously the Holy Spirit took over to give you the words needed to act appropriately. You certainly experienced danger. I'm relieved that it turned out the way it did, and that you weren't harmed. You are certainly not in trouble with me, but I want to make sure that you're not in danger. The devil has a habit of not going away when thwarted. And for that reason, I want you to remain silent about this encounter, and to check back in with me regularly, so that I know you're OK."

Priests often share sermons with each other; we tell stories about funny things that happen at coffee hour; we sometimes even relate an embarrassing mistake made during a worship service. But one of the most important experiences of my ordained ministry had just happened, and the bishop had cautioned me to tell no one about it. I couldn't pick up the phone and tell my best friend: "Guess what? I cast out a demon by calling on the name of Jesus."

Visit to a Korean Grandmother

Most of the families in the St. Mary's Korean congregation were multi-generational. The parents both worked, usually in a family-owned business, and the grandmother (occasionally a grandfather) remained at home in charge of the household, the meals, and the care of their grandchildren.

Every family continued to speak Korean, or Hangul, at home. The parents learned barely enough English to get by running their businesses. The grandchildren, attending local public schools, developed English language skills, becoming fluent in English rapidly, especially since many school systems simply immersed immigrant children into regular classrooms, rather than develop and segregate these children into ESL classes. The grandparents, having little social contact beyond the family, seldom learned to speak English.

As an integral part of my ministry, I made weekly visits to the homes of families in my congregations. These visits helped me develop relationships with the children and their grandparents, and the visits also gave me the opportunity to immerse myself in the Korean language and culture. In the early days of my ministry when my language skills were sparse at best, I relied upon the young children in the family to serve as translators when I brought communion to their grandparents.

I timed my visits to ensure that the elementary school children were home from school, announcing my arrival as I removed my shoes at the front door. The children always ran to greet me, all talking at once to tell me about their school day, as we moved to the kitchen where Grandmother, in anticipation of my visit, prepared food. I learned early on that I could not refuse these meals, and so the kitchen became the locus of my visits, and Grandmother's cooking often served as my primary meal of the day. The children busily translated our conversation, as I tried to communicate with Grandmother.

After the meal, we all adjourned to the living room, or sometimes to Grandmother's bedroom, and I would pray for her and administer the bread and wine of Holy Communion. Since the children translated for me, I often asked them to offer additional prayers and join me when I laid hands on their grandmother.

One afternoon, as I drove to a family's home in the suburbs, traffic stood at a standstill. I arrived at the home almost an hour later than usual. When I rang the doorbell, the children ran to the door as usual, but they greeted me:

"You don't have to pray for *Halmeoni* (Grandmother) or for her back to feel better. We were afraid you weren't coming today, so we already laid hands on her and prayed for God to heal her."

I thought I had been coming to their home each week to practice my language skills and to give my pastoral care. Unbeknownst to me, I had also been making disciples.

The Miracle

A woman in the congregation flew to Seoul for a hysterectomy. I assumed she had traveled for surgery to receive aftercare from family members who still lived in her native home. A man complained of arthritic knees but resisted any suggestion of surgery. I assumed he thought he couldn't be away from his store for weeks of rehab. I couldn't understand why parents were not taking children to doctors for routine check-ups or annual shots, until Mary had been struck by a speeding car while riding her bicycle. Then I became aware of the reality. Most Korean immigrants were without medical insurance.

The fire department ambulance took Mary to the hospital. Bad news! Her leg had suffered a compound fracture, requiring a number of surgeries to align the broken bones and place pins for healing, months of rehab to walk again. At sixteen, her future suddenly looked bleak. Mary lay in the hospital emergency room awaiting surgery. Her injuries were too serious to fly her to Seoul for medical care. Where to find the money to pay for her medical care here in Chicago? The men in the congregation leapt into action. They began their own congregational "Gofundme" campaign, each family pledging what they could to help pay for Mary's medical expenses.

The phone rang to convey the news about Mary. As I prepared to leave for the hospital, Mary's brother Paul called to ask me to pick up members of the youth group and take them to the hospital with me. I drove to the church and started the church van. Driving throughout the northwest suburbs, I picked up members of the youth group as I did most Sunday evenings, and we headed to the hospital.

Shooing away the nurse who tried to tell us we could only visit with her two at a time, six of her youth group companions and I surrounded Mary's bed. Heavily sedated, she managed a smile as one friend took her hand. Another began to rub her forehead. Paul laid his hands on her leg. Soon all pairs of hands were hovering over her wounds. The group began to pray, reminding Jesus how he had cured the man born blind, Jairus' daughter, the lame man by the side of the pool. They urged Jesus for another miracle. Their fervent prayers implored God to cure their beloved Mary. My own prayers seemed almost superfluous as I listened to the faithful expressions of her friends. The nurse who had tried to limit visitors now stood quietly at the door, captivated by what she observed, and making no move to get us to leave. Mary's eyes closed. Our prayers concluded. We returned to the van for our trip back to each youth member's home.

The next morning, I received a call from Mary's father. His voice sounded astonished: his words spilling out in both English and Korean. Mary had been taken for an MRI before the first surgery, and the doctors could hardly believe, much less report, what they saw. Overnight, Mary's leg bones, shattered and displaced by her accident, had realigned perfectly and were already beginning to knit together. The doctors cast her leg for support, and she went home that afternoon. No surgery. No thousands of dollars in medical bills. No extensive rehab.

Who says miracles only took place thousands of years ago when Jesus walked the shores of Galilee? The unquestioning faith of a group of teenagers certainly refuted my doubts.

Christmas in Alaska

After years of juggling family gatherings and multiple church services at Christmastime, I found myself with no obligations – no children at home – no sermons to prepare for the upcoming Christmas. It felt strange not to be needed. And then came the phone call from Mark MacDonald, Episcopal Bishop of Alaska. "I'm wondering if you might be interested in coming here to Alaska over Christmas break. I need a priest to go to Ft. Yukon for a couple of weeks. The village has been without a priest for some time, and there's no spare priest here I can send. I'd love for you to spend Christmas in the village, doing the Christmas services, and catching up on the pastoral care, baptisms, and weddings – hopefully, not too many funerals."

A chance to be useful. Another chance to be a missionary again – to preach the message of Christ to "others" of a different culture. I had first heard the call to be a missionary on that hillside in Hokkaido as a teenager. After leaving Korean ministry to teach at the seminary, I had another chance to be a missionary again – even if only for a few weeks. And in Alaska – quite literally bringing the light of Christ into the land of darkness.

But the bishop's invitation didn't come with funding. I'd have to raise money for the trip. I'd need a plane ticket and heavy winter clothing. I shared the bishop's invitation with some members of my home parish, St. Gregory's Church. They responded immediately. One parishioner pledged air mileage for my plane tickets. Another church member bought me a pair of Sorel boots. A former marine lent me her arctic jacket, issued to her when she'd been stationed in Alaska. Gloves, wool socks, thermal underwear appeared overnight. In an earlier conversation, the bishop lamented the need to upgrade the diocesan computers. I mentioned this need to a friend who had a computer shop, and he began to collect parts for me to take. On my way to Alaska! To a small outpost above the arctic circle! A chance to be a missionary once again!!

I stood in line to board the United flight to Anchorage, having checked one suitcase of winter clothes and clergy vestments and a second suitcase filled with 50 pounds of computer parts. We arrived in Anchorage at breakfast time but in total darkness. The sun began to rise over the horizon, then set again as if it couldn't quite make it. The unfulfilled promise of dawn. No real daylight. Alaska in winter.

I spent the first couple of days visiting churches in Anchorage with the bishop and repairing computers. Then on to Fairbanks to spend several days at the diocesan center. I stayed at the MacDonalds' home for several days to work at the diocesan center. I walked from the bishop's home to the center - every inch of my body, including my face - covered against the minus 20-degree temperature. But drivers in Alaska always stop to pick up pedestrians along the roadside, so I usually got offered a ride.

Time to head to Ft. Yukon, a small village on the Yukon River, straddling the Arctic Circle. Population about 500, mostly Gwich'in (Athabaskan) natives. In summer I might have cruised up the river, but in winter a twelve-passenger propeller-driven airplane provided the only access. As I prepared to board the plane, I stood on a scale with my luggage, as the pilot calculated the total weight of passengers and luggage. Then the crew added chickens and vegetables until they reached the plane's weight limit. Our pilot looked too young to have a driver's license, much less fly a plane. I tried to calm my fears and queasy stomach. Surely God, having chosen me to make this trip, wouldn't let me die enroute.

The ride was the longest hour of my life. Finally, the plane glided onto a snowy surface. I couldn't detect an actual runway. A villager met me on a snowmobile to transport me to the village. The coldest and scariest ten-minute ride of my life – racing in a vehicle I'd never been on before. I felt unstable, my legs straddling the snowmobile behind the driver, trying to hold onto her jacket for dear life, fearing we'd crash at any moment. I deposited my belongings in a small cabin next to St. Stephen's Church – my home for the next two weeks. My chauffeur informed me: "Grandmother is waiting." The village's oldest resident had heard the plane land and awaited my arrival. No chance to warm up. No time to rest.

I gathered what I needed for a communion service and climbed back onto the snowmobile. We stopped in front of a one-room shack. Smoke came from the chimney. I stepped inside. An old woman wrapped in blankets sat beside the woodstove, her hands outstretched, awaiting "The Body of Christ." And I, the missionary, bringing Christ into that humble darkness.

Christmas Eve. There had been other attempts at missionary work in Ft. Yukon, but St. Stephen's remained the major church in the village. Family after family crammed into the little church - as if every villager yearned to celebrate Christmas Mass. My heart overflowed. Without me, the visiting priest, they could not celebrate Christmas.

The service over, villagers back in their homes. I crawled into the bunk bed in the cabin, still shivering, a jacket over my pj's to keep warm. Too many thoughts about the events of that day to fall asleep immediately. And what about tomorrow morning? Another church service, but would anyone come? It seemed as if every villager had already come to church for their Christmas communion that night.

As I lay in bed, I heard rumbling and roaring sounds. Like dozens of snowmobiles revving their engines. Were the villagers partying in the snow? The next morning, I learned the sounds were travelers coming into the village. The word had spread: a priest at St. Stephen's. Trappers and traders along the river spent the night traveling to be at St. Stephen's on Christmas morning. The next few days blurred. Children being baptized. Visits to bless families and homes. Two weddings. The Light of Christ in this land of darkness.

But tragedy also struck on Christmas. Deprived of their native, historical and cultural ways of earning a living by fishing and trapping, most Athabaskan men were on the government "dole." They sat in the government-provided recreational center. They gambled; they drank. And they died. Three alcohol related deaths: a teenager succumbed to a snowmobile wreck, a young man took his own life, an old man died of liver failure. Three funerals. Anticipating inevitable deaths, men of the village dug graves in the summer, filled them with straw in preparation for burying the dead in winter. The sad but grace-filled part of a priest's ministry.

Three weeks flew by. Back home in Illinois, a friend asked, "How do people in Alaska survive with no sunshine for months at a time?" Although the sun didn't really shine during that Christmas in Alaska, the Son – the light of Christ – illuminated every place, every person, every experience.

Good Friday Reflection
*(A Reflection first given at the Good Friday morning
church service on April 14, 2014 at St. Gregory's
Episcopal Church, Deerfield, Illinois)*

It had only been a couple of weeks since
my son Charlie had died. The funeral was
over and I had returned home, but my grief
was still deep and very raw. The telephone
rang, and immediately I recognized the
voice on the other end of line: "Hello,
Meredith, this is Frank."

Bishop Frank Griswold had been my
bishop, my pastor, and my confessor. He
had ordained me to the priesthood. No
longer Bishop of Chicago, he was now the
Presiding Bishop of the Episcopal Church.
Yet when word reached him in New York
that my son had died, he called me to offer

his condolences, his prayers, and what turned out to be a life-changing insight. As we talked ,he asked me a question that no one else, not even my closest priest friends had asked. "How is your faith holding up?"

I began to cry as I responded, "I feel like Martha. I believe in the resurrection of the dead and life everlasting. I just can't get there." As we talked more, I found myself telling him that I just couldn't get to Easter. I found myself stuck on Good Friday. There was a silence on the other end of the phone line. Then the Bishop said, "But that's where you need to be right now. Easter will come! But right now, your task is simply to join Mary at the foot of the cross and weep."

The years have gone by, and my son's death has become part of the rhythm and fabric of my life. But I have never forgotten that conversation with my bishop. I think about it in particular each year on this day. Easter will soon be upon us. Once again, we will welcome God's most precious gift to humankind. We will shout our Hallelujahs and rejoice that Christ is risen indeed. But not today. Today we cannot anticipate what is to come; we dare not even hope. Today all we can do is join Mary at the foot of the cross and weep.

*M*usical *M*usings

Through the front doors of Jubilation and onto the bus for the ten-minute ride to downtown Fredericksburg. Crowds filled Market Square but the blue folding chairs belonging to Jubilation were set up – four rows - right in front of the steps where the band was setting up. I sat down in the second row on the aisle. Did I want a gelato? Still full from dinner, I decided to wait. While the band, "Shades of Grey," warmed up, a senior couple began to dance at the foot of the steps, creating a makeshift dance floor. They wore matching purple shirts and white shorts. They were younger and much more spry than I (but everyone is younger and often more spry than I these days). They danced as if they were contestants on *Dancing with the Stars.* I could hardly believe how skilled, how talented, how musical, how in sync they were with each other. They had probably been dancing together for fifty years. They gave the word "compatibility" new meaning. They obviously enjoyed each other, but they also enjoyed the attention they were getting from us – their captive audience.

The Square became more and more crowded. After a brief introduction from the disc jockey of the local radio station, the band began to play. At first the "purple and white couple" were the only ones on the dance floor. The crowd sang along. Children ran to and fro. The line grew longer for gelatos – and also for beer on the other side of the Square. One by one, children began to run up and down, jumping around the dance floor. Another couple joined the purple and white couple. Several young women on the upper steps began to stomp their feet and clap in tune with the music. People continued to flow into the Square, setting down folding chairs. A woman picked up her young son and began to twirl him in tune with the music. Slowly, the dance floor area began to fill with people – dancing alone – dancing with partners – dancing with friends and children. One man swung his daughter over his head, her squeals rising above the band sounds. A young college-aged man tried to dance with two young women at once – keeping beat with neither. His companions gave up on him and danced together as he shuffled his feet and swung his arms back and forth out of rhythm with them and the music. The area in front of the stage filled with people – young and old – gyrating to the music. Dance styles from several decades.

I looked around at my Jubilation friends. A number of the men had canes hanging across their laps. A woman whom I often saw dancing at such events seemed content to mouth the words of the song as she clapped her hands. No one rose to dance. I thought about my move to Jubilation. The yoga classes. My stained-glass studio. The water aerobics classes. So many neighbors and friends. My apartment which displayed my precious antiques. My companion cat Cupcake, who enjoyed sleeping on the balcony. Such a great decision to move to Fredericksburg. My life was so good. But I sure could use a dance partner.

Sweet Ninety

"See you in August, Grandma"–My first clue. Other hints to the event followed. No one confirmed my suspicions. No one offered me any details. But I figured out that my sister and brother from Denver were coming. My son asked me for a cousin's address. I learned that a grandson and his family had booked the guest suite here at Jubilation for my birthday weekend, when the concierge called me to confirm "dates my guests would be here." My best friend, who always celebrates my birthday with me, booked her plane ticket from Illinois. A surprise party -- definitely in the works. Well, not exactly a total surprise –

but I didn't know what, where, or exactly when.

On Friday night, August 9, my son Barry and his wife Monica picked me up to go to the baseball game across the street at the FredNats Stadium. They brought a special shirt for me to wear. I reminded them that I already had a FredNats shirt, but they appeared with a red shirt embroidered with "Potter 90th Birthday." I put on the shirt, and we walked across the parking lot and down the path to the stadium entrance. I spotted two grandsons and their families from Denver. A granddaughter and her family. My middle son all the way from Milwaukee. The grandson and his family, who had booked the Jubilation guest suite. Grown grandchildren from here in Virginia. I hugged one great grandchild after another. I soon counted 28 family members. We took our seats. The night air, hot and muggy. Bugs everywhere. The family all waved paper fans announcing my birthday.

Lots of swatting the flying bugs. Lots of conversations. Lots of shouting at runs and foul balls. At the middle of the 8th inning, a camera man appeared, pointing his camera at me. I looked up at the stadium's huge Megatron and saw the announcement: "Happy 90th Birthday, Meredith Potter." I waved at the camera, as two dozen family members also waved their fans and shouted happy birthday.

Saturday morning, August 10. Ninety years old! I couldn't believe it. I didn't feel 90. How could all those years have gone by? I thought about the important events of my life. The grandchildren and great grandchildren. The baptisms. The weddings. The death of my son.

I shared breakfast with my best friend and the Connecticut grandchildren and great grandchildren staying at Jubilation. After breakfast, the great grandchildren left to swim in our outdoor pool. No mention of a birthday gathering. At eleven o'clock, we went downstairs to the lobby. Monica, who turned the grandchildren's desire for a reunion into reality, had decorated the entire lounge. Swarms of loved ones there to greet me. Balloons. Birthday cards. Gift bags. More friends from Illinois. My cousin. My siblings and their spouses. Friends from here at Jubilation. The staff prepared a wonderful lunch outside under the tent for family and friends. Mid-afternoon found me splashing in the pool with nine great grandchildren!!

Sunday the church congregation doubled in size as dozens of family members joined the service. Another great gathering with my church family hosting a meal downstairs after the service.

A huge gathering of family and friends to celebrate my life. Kind of what I imagine my funeral will be, except the difference – I was there, alive and in person to celebrate with them.

As I look back at the glorious weekend gathering, I reflect on the experiences of my life. Many stories I've written about in this book. The reader can count the years better than I. How did I get to be ninety? I exercise, walk, do yoga and water aerobics, and my body feels 60. I study Hebrew, write short stories, and play bridge, and my mind feels 30. The mathematician within me calculates: 60+30. That's the ninety I want to be.

I know this about my life: I am so loved. I am so blessed. Ninety wonderful years. Sweet ninety indeed.

Meredith Woods Potter spent her formative years in post-World War II Japan, returning to the U.S. to attend college. In her mid-thirties she entered graduate school as a single mother of four boys, earning advanced degrees in mathematics. She became a college professor, published researcher in forest fire behavior, and founded the computer science department at Rockford College. In her late forties, she left academia to pursue her childhood call to become an Episcopal priest. Over the next three decades, she served the Episcopal Church in parish ministry and held several leadership positions in ministry for Asian Americans. An engaging preacher, a number of her sermons have been published, including a Christmas collection titled *The Priceless Gift: Stories of Christmas.* She now lives in Fredericksburg, Virginia, where she enjoys writing, studying Hebrew and creating stained-glass art.

www.ingramcontent.com/pod-product-compliance
Lightning Source LLC
Chambersburg PA
CBHW020254130626
46549CB00005B/2213